Revise your Sounds

You can practise writing them but you don't have to do them all at once!

Colour the tree!

3

Zz

It is a beautiful spring day and Bee and her friend from the hive are busy collecting pollen. They fly from flower to flower, buzzing 'zzzzzzzzz' as they go. Bee lands in the middle of a big soft flower and sits down. "It's time for a rest," she buzzes, "Zzzz."

Colour the picture!

NOW YOU CAN

Do the action and say the sound!

Action
Put your arms out at your sides and flap them like a bee, saying **ZZZzzzzZZZ.**

Which of these things have the sound 'z' in them?
Join them to the letter 'z'.

NOW YOU CAN
Write the letter.
Start at the top!
Try different
colours!

Inky says,
"Hold your
pencil
correctly!"

💡 Tips for Parents

Remember to call 'z' by its sound 'zzz' and not its name 'zed'.

5

BUZZING BEES

Starting at the bee, buzz your pencil to every flower with a 'z' sou
in it and practise writing the letter.

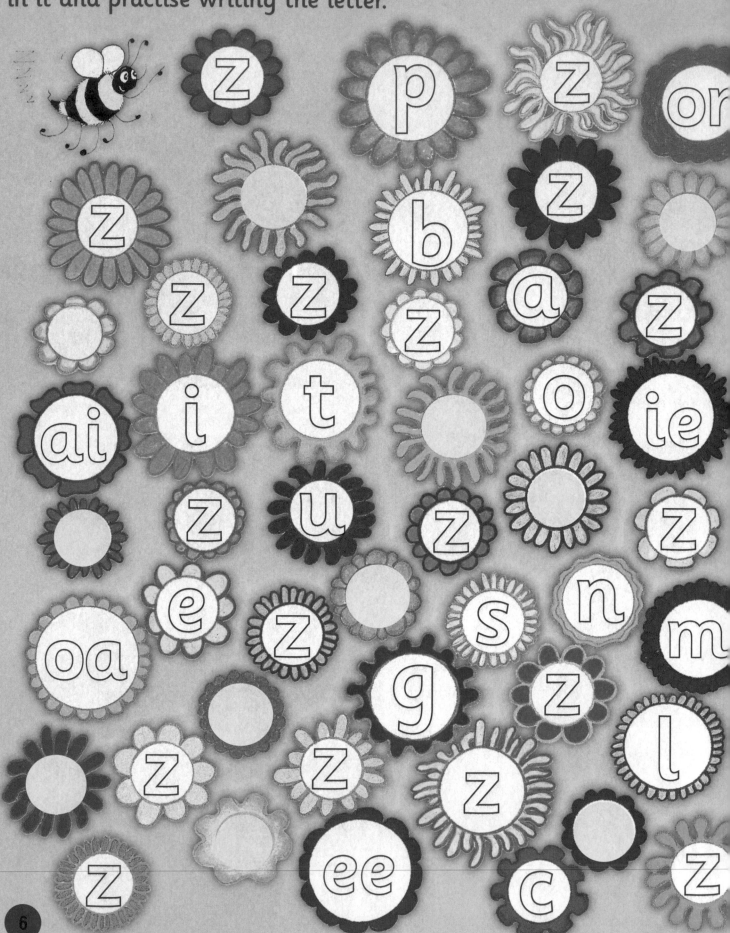

Vowel Forest

Say the word, listen for the missing vowel sound and write it in.

ai **ee** **ie** **oa** **or**

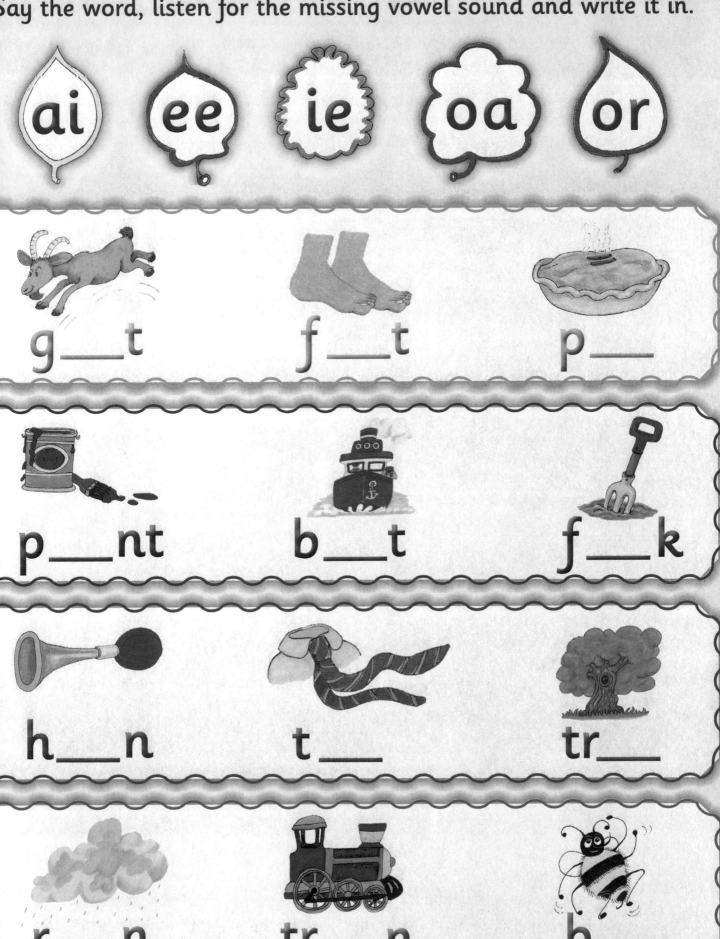

g__t f__t p____

p__nt b__t f__k

h__n t____ tr____

r__n tr__n b____

W w

Bee lies in the middle of the soft flower and watch the clouds float by. She thinks one of the clouds loo like a big face. "It is probably the west wind blowir the clouds along," she laughs. Bee blows at the clou too, pretending she is the wind - w, w, w. "I could st here all day," she buzzes happily.

Colour the picture!

NOW YOU CA

Do the action and say the sound!

Action
Blow onto your open hand, as if you are the wind, and say *wh, wh, wh.*

Which of these things have the sound 'w' in them?
Join them to the letter 'w'.

OW YOU CAN

Write the letter.
Start at the top!
Try different colours!

Inky says,
"Try writing
'w' in one
go!"

9

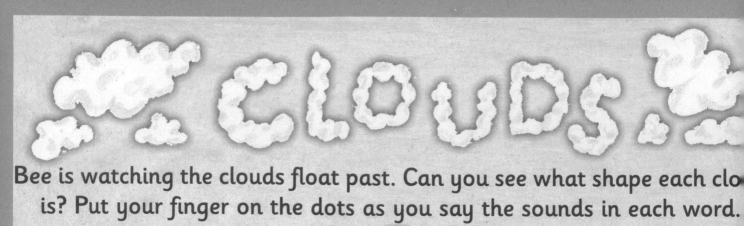

CLOUDS

Bee is watching the clouds float past. Can you see what shape each cloud is? Put your finger on the dots as you say the sounds in each word.

Words like 't-r-ee' and 'b-oa-t' only have 3 sounds.

Make a Windmill

1. Cut out a square of paper and decorate it on both sides.

2. Fold it in half diagonally along the facing corners and then in half again.

3. Cut from each corner to halfway along the folded line.

4. Take the top left hand corner of one quarter and fold it into the middle, holding it there with your thumb.

5. Fold each alternate corner down.

6. Put a split pin through the points and the back.

NOW YOU CAN

Use the windmill shape to make flowers!

Read the animal stickers and stick them on the correct pens.

Colour the pictures!

ng

As Bee is lying on the flower she hears a strange 'ng, ng, ng' sound. She goes to investigate and finds Snake pretending to be a weightlifter, trying to lift a heavy piece of wood and making a strange 'ng' noise. "Why are you making that funny 'ng' noise?" asks Bee. "That's the noise weightlifters make!" replies Snake.

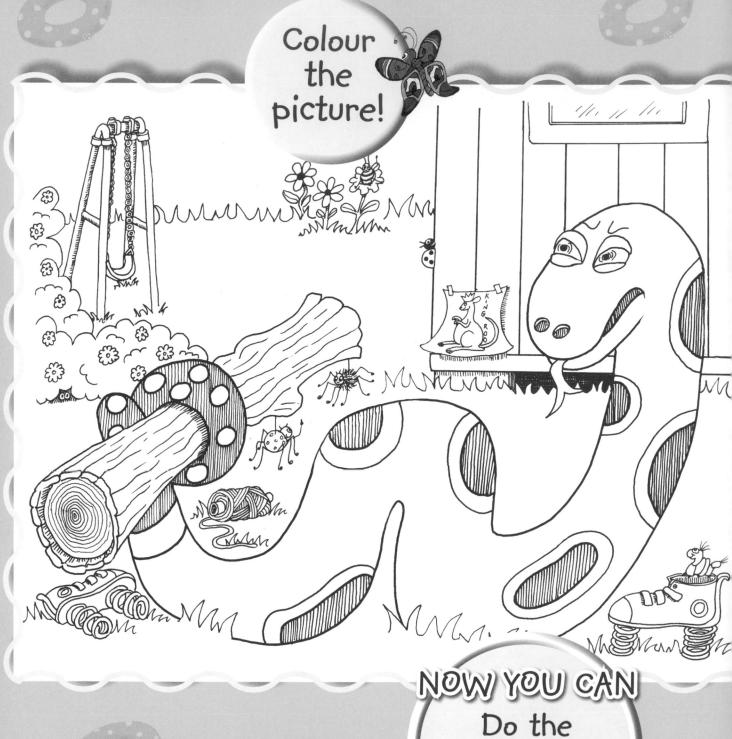

Colour the picture!

NOW YOU CAN
Do the action and say the sound!

Action
Imagine you are a weightlifter, and pretend to lift a heavy weight above your head, saying *ng...*

Which of these things have the sound 'ng' in them?
Join them to the 'ng'.

OW YOU CAN
rite the letters.
Start on the dot
and join the
letters.

Inky says,
"Try writing
'ng' all
joined-up!"

ng ng ng

ng ng ng

Tips for Parents

When joining 'n' and 'g', write the 'n' as usual, then take the joining tail over
to where the 'g' starts, STOP, come back and do caterpillar 'c' to start the 'g'.

15

WORD WEIGHTS

NOW YOU CAN
Read the word and circle the correct picture to match.

sing

3 tree

duck

green

flag

well

zebra

horn

16

Add a Vowel

OW YOU CAN
Make some words using the vowel sounds below.

a e i
o u

How many different words can you make?

p	n	p	n	p	n
b	d	b	d	b	d
h	t	h	t	h	t
f	n	f	n	f	n

| a | a | a | a | e | e | i |
| i | i | o | o | o | u | u |

17

Anagrams

NOW YOU CAN

Unscramble the letters to make a word.

Write the words next to the pictures.

b e w

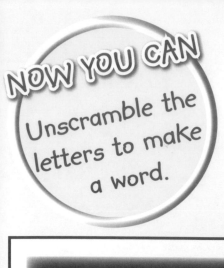
_ _ _

l w l e

_ _ _ _

n i r g

_ _ _ _

w i s m

_ _ _ _

f o r g

_ _ _ _

r z b e a

_ _ _ _

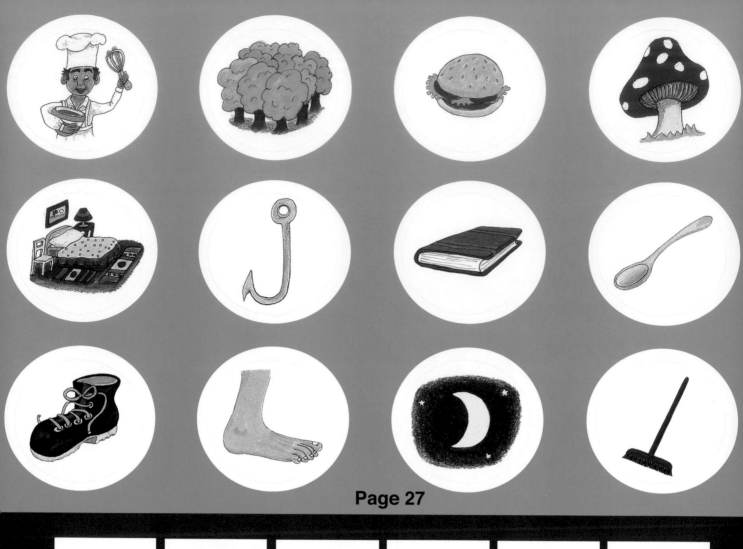

Page 27

Pages 22 & 23

snails	zebras	bees
goats	frog	rabbits
wombat	crabs	skunks
panda	bats	**Pages 12 & 13**

Develop the Photos

Help Inky develop the photos she has taken.

ring

sing

Read the word and draw the picture.

wing

king

sting

swing

Vv

Suddenly there is a loud vvvvvvv sound as a van pul[ls] up outside the house. Bee and Snake hurry off to se[e] who it is. Inky is already there. "It's Zack and Jess[']s Uncle Vic," whispers Inky. "He's taken a parcel insid[e]. Come on, let's see what it is." "I'm going to be a va[n] driver!" shouts Bee. "Vvvvvvv."

Colour the picture!

VAL'S FRUIT & VEG

OPEN

MUSIC

vic's VAN DELIVERIES

555 VIC

NOW YOU CAN

Do the action and say the sound!

Action
Pretend to turn the steering wheel of a van and say *VVVVvvvVVV*.

Which of these things have the sound 'v' in them?
Join them to the letter 'v'.

NOW YOU CAN
Write the letter.
Start at the top!
Try different colours!

Inky says, "Hold your pencil correctly!"

21

f

ai

p

t

oa

g

ee

l

ck

r

i

or

oo

Uncle Vic has bought Zack and Jess a present from h[is]
holiday in Switzerland. It is a cuckoo clock. Uncle V[ic]
moves the long hand so it points to the twelve, an[d]
out pops a cuckoo from the little door at the top of th[e]
clock, oo-**oo** , oo-**oo** , oo-**oo** . Bee, Inky and Snak[e]
love the cuckoo clock and spend the afternoon bein[g]
cuckoos until they are tired out.

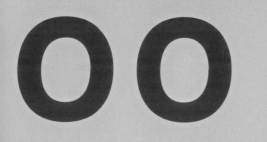

Colour the picture!

NOW YOU CAN
Do the action and say the sound!

Action
Move your head back and forth, like the cuckoo in a cuckoo clock, calling *u oo; u oo.*

Which of these things have one of the 'oo' sounds in them? Join them to the 'oo'.

NOW YOU CAN
Write the letters. Start on the dot and join the letters.

Inky says, "Hold your pencil correctly!"

💡 **Tips for Parents**
When joining 'o' and 'o', write the first 'o' as usual, then go straight across, STOP, come back and do caterpillar 'c' to start the next 'o'.

25

Make a Cuckoo Clock

1 Cut out the clock pieces and cut the slit in the doorway.

2 Push the cuckoo through the doorway.

3 Add the clock hands, using a split pin to fasten them.

4 Push the cuckoo in and out, saying oo-oo, oo-oo.

Colour the clock first!

26

uckoo Clocks

W YOU CAN
ad the words
and find the
stickers that
match.

Try
00
and
OO

Put your
stickers on
the clock
faces.

book

moon

boot

cook

hook

foot

wood

food

broom

bedroom

spoon

toadstool

Sound Cards

ng oo

w oo

z v

as flashcards

find the sound

copy & play pairs or sn

make & blend wor

Tips for Parents

Cut out each card and use them in the ways suggested. Keep them and add them to the sound cards in the other activity books.

Match the Words

cup

buzz

plum

wet

van

wind

well

jam

vet

jet

jump

zoo

jug

snip

wag

Word and Picture Matching

NOW YOU CAN
Join the words to the pictures and later you can cut out and match.

pen

cap

hip

cat

web	
zebra	
van	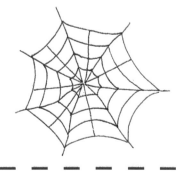
ring	

30

💡 Tips for Parents

These are words using the sounds learnt so far.

swing	
book	
foot	
moon	
boot	
zoo	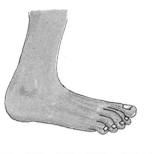

Put your stickers on the empty squares.

NOW YOU CAN
Find the stickers that match the sentences.

Sentences

Sentences start with a capital letter and end with a full stop.

Ss   Ff   Aa   Bb   Ss   Aa   Ff   Bb

A big goat runs.

Frogs can hop.

A hen sits on a nest.

Ben and Sam got we

FRONT COVERS

Look at the picture on the front cover of each book and complete the word underneath by writing the final sound.

re_

cu_

ha_

do_

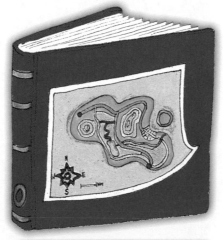
ma_

su_

b__

rai_

ri__

33

Practise Writing the Letters

Start on the dot and try to stay inside the lines!

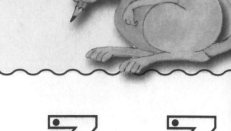

z z z z z z

w w w w w w

ng ng ng ng

v v v v v v

oo oo oo oo

34